Presented to

by

on

BIBLE
for little hearts

Illustrated by Elena Kucharik

Tyndale House Publishers, Inc.
WHEATON, ILLINOIS

© 1995 by Tyndale House Publishers. All rights reserved.
Illustrations © 1995 by Elena Kucharik. All rights reserved.
Little Blessings is a trademark of Tyndale House Publishers, Inc.
The *Little Blessings* characters are a trademark of Elena Kucharik.

Compiled by the Livingstone Corporation.
Prayers by James C. Galvin.

Scripture quotations on pages 13, 17, 19, 31, 35, 47, 49, 51, 57, 61,
and 71 are taken from the *Holy Bible*, New International Version®. NIV®.
Copyright © 1973, 1978, 1984 by International Bible Society. Used by
permission of Zondervan Publishing House. All rights reserved.

Scripture quotations on pages 7, 9, 11, 15, 21, 27, 33, 43, 45, 59, and 65 are
taken from *The Living Bible*, copyright © 1971 owned by assignment by
KNT Charitable Trust. All rights reserved.

Scripture quotations on pages 23, 25, 29, 37, 39, 41, 53, 55, and 63 are
taken from the New Revised Standard Version of the Bible, copyrighted,
1989 by the Division of Christian Education of the National Council of the
Churches of Christ in the United States of America, and are used by permission. All rights reserved.

Library of Congress Cataloging-in-Publication Data

Bible. English. Selections. 1995.
    Bible for Little Hearts / [compiled by the Livingstone Corporation ;
prayers by James C. Galvin].
        p. cm.
    ISBN 0-8423-1306-0
    1. Children—Prayer-books and devotions—English. [1. Prayer books
and devotions.] I. Galvin, James C. II. Livingstone Corporation. III. Title.
BS391.2.L49 1995
220.5'2—dc20   94-9694

Printed in the United States of America

01 00 99 98
10 9 8 7 6

The most valuable present you can offer a child is a love for God's Word. Whether you purchased this Bible or received it as a gift, you will find it a useful tool for introducing your child to the Bible.

Bible for Little Hearts is not Bible stories, but a collection of favorite Bible passages intended to give comfort and encouragement to you and your child. The endearing art of illustrator Elena Kucharik helps to reinforce the messages from the Bible.

Keep this Bible near your baby's crib or on display as a continual reminder of your responsibility to teach your child about God. As your child develops an interest in picture books, keep this in the book pile. After reading it over and over, your child will start to learn these verses by heart. You may also find this book to be a handy collection of memory verses when your child is no longer a baby.

May the Lord bless you and your child as you explore and learn to love God's Word.

For Mom

Honor your father and

mother, that you may

have a long, good life.

EXODUS 20:12

Yes, be bold and strong! . . . For remember, the Lord your God is with you wherever you go.

JOSHUA 1:9

9

The Lord gives his own

reward for doing good

and for being loyal.

1 SAMUEL 26:23

11

O Lord, our Lord, how

majestic is your name

in all the earth!

PSALM 8:9

Because the Lord is

my Shepherd, I have

everything I need!

PSALM 23:1

Surely goodness and love will follow me all the days of my life, and I will dwell in the house of the Lord forever.

PSALM 23:6

When I am afraid,

I will trust in you.

PSALM 56:3

I love the Lord because

he hears my prayers and

answers them.

PSALM 116:1

O give thanks to the Lord, for he is good; his steadfast love endures forever!

PSALM 118:1

23

I praise you, for I am

fearfully and wonderfully

made.

PSALM 139:14

In everything you do,

put God first, and he will

direct you and crown

your efforts with success.

PROVERBS 3:6

But those who wait for the Lord shall renew their strength, they shall mount up with wings like eagles, they shall run and not be weary, they shall walk and not faint.

ISAIAH 40:31

29

"For I know the plans I have for you," declares the Lord, "plans to prosper you and not to harm you, plans to give you hope and a future."

JEREMIAH 29:11

Great is his faithfulness;

his loving-kindness

begins afresh each day.

LAMENTATIONS 3:23

I will give you a new

heart and put a new

spirit in you.

EZEKIEL 36:26

35

God, the Lord, is my

strength.

HABAKKUK 3:19

In everything do to others as you would have them do to you.

MATTHEW 7:12

Jesus said, "For where two or three are gathered in my name, I am there among them."

MATTHEW 18:20

41

Then Jesus took the

children into his arms

and placed his hands on

their heads and he

blessed them.

MARK 10:16

For God loved the world

so much that he gave his

only Son so that anyone

who believes in him shall

not perish but have

eternal life.

JOHN 3:16

Believe in the Lord Jesus, and you will be saved—you and your household.

ACTS 16:31

Therefore, if anyone is in Christ, he is a new creation; the old has gone, the new has come!

2 CORINTHIANS 5:17

49

But the fruit of the

Spirit is love, joy, peace,

patience, kindness,

goodness, faithfulness,

gentleness and self-control.

GALATIANS 5:22-23

51

Children, obey your

parents in the Lord, for

this is right.

EPHESIANS 6:1

I can do all things

through him who

strengthens me.

PHILIPPIANS 4:13

And my God will meet

all your needs according

to his glorious riches in

Christ Jesus.

PHILIPPIANS 4:19

The whole Bible was

given to us by

inspiration from God ...;

it straightens us out and

helps us do what is right.

2 TIMOTHY 3:16

Everyone should be quick to listen, slow to speak and slow to become angry.

JAMES 1:19

But the word of the

Lord endures forever.

1 PETER 1:25

See how very much our heavenly Father loves us, for he allows us to be called his children.

1 JOHN 3:1

Prayers

Many parents wonder when it is the best time to teach their children to pray. Children learn to pray by hearing us pray and by praying with us. Even before the infant can understand your words, it is important for YOU to pray with your child so that you are in the habit of praying together each day. Together you can thank Jesus for what the baby's about to eat. When you lay your sleeping infant in the crib, say a good-night prayer even though your child is asleep. Parents who do this don't have to worry about when to start prayer with their children. They will also have the comfort of knowing they have prayed for and with their child for his or her entire life. It's never too early to begin praying with your child. Here are a few prayers to get you started.

A BEDTIME PRAYER

Dear God,

Thank you for this day.

Thank you for keeping me safe.

Please help me to fall asleep soon.

I love you.

In Jesus' name, amen.

A WAKE-UP PRAYER

Good morning, God!

Thank you for today.

Thank you for the beautiful things

you have made.

Help me to do what I know is right.

I trust in you.

In Jesus' name, amen.

A MEALTIME PRAYER

Dear God,

Thank you for my food.

Thank you for all the good things

you give me.

In Jesus' name, amen.

THE LORD'S PRAYER

Our Father in heaven,

hallowed be your name,

your kingdom come,

your will be done

on earth as it is in heaven.

Give us today our daily bread.

Forgive us our debts,

as we also have forgiven our debtors.

And lead us not into temptation,

but deliver us from the evil one.

MATTHEW 6:9-13

THANK YOU FOR MY FRIENDS

Dear God,

Thank you for my friends.

Please help me to be kind to them.

Help me to be fair and not cheat.

In Jesus' name, amen.

THANK YOU FOR MY PARENTS

Dear Father in heaven,

Thank you for my parents.

Help me to do what they tell me to,

even when I don't feel like it.

In Jesus' name, amen.

THANK YOU FOR THE BIBLE

Dear God,

Thank you for the Bible.

Help me to read it so I can know and

do what you want me to.

Thank you for sending Jesus

to save us.

In Jesus' name, amen.

HELP ME TO PRAY EVERY DAY

Dear God,

I love you.

Thank you for your great power.

Thank you that I can talk to you.

Help me to pray every day.

In Jesus' name, amen.

Forgive Me When I Do Bad Things

Dear God,

Please forgive me when

I do bad things.

Help me to want your way

and not just my own.

Thank you for what I can do to

make other people happy.

In Jesus' name, amen.

HELP ME WHEN I'M AFRAID

Dear God,

Thank you for caring about

how I feel.

Please help me not to be afraid.

Thank you for being with me

all the time.

In Jesus' name, amen.